# KRISTOFFERSEN

# NOR SHALL YOUR GLORY BE FORGOT

## AN ESSAY IN PHOTOGRAPHS

Introduction by
Brian C. Pohanka

St. Martin's Press
New York

*Nor Shall Your Glory Be Forgot*
Copyright © 1999 by Kris Kristoffersen
Introduction © 1999 by Brian C. Pohanka
All rights reserved.
Printed in Great Britain.
Designed by MW Productions, NYC in association with Lundquist Design, NYC

No part of this book may be used or reproduced in any manner whatsoever without written
permission except in the case of brief quotations embodied in critical articles or reviews.

For information, address St. Martin's Press, 175 Fifth Avenue, New York, N.Y. 10010.

Library of Congress Cataloging-in-Publication Data

Kristoffersen.
    Nor shall your glory be forgot : an essay in photographs /
Kristoffersen; introduction by Brian C. Pohanka.—1st ed.
        p.    cm.
    ISBN 0-312-20473-6
    1. United States—History—Civil War, 1861–1865—Campaigns—
Pictorial works.   2. Historical reenactments—United States—
Pictorial works.   3. United States—History—Civil War, 1861–1865—
Campaigns.   I. Pohanka, Brian C., 1956– .   II. Title.
E470.K95  1999
973.7'3'00222—dc21                                              99-10694
                                                                    CIP

First Edition: May 1999

10 9 8 7 6 5 4 3 2 1

# Foreword by Kristoffersen

To me, the intriguing questions about the Civil War are a series of "what ifs?". What if Lee had won at Gettysburg? What if Grant had lost at Shiloh? What if Lincoln had a great commander at the start of the war? What if, what if? Well, while we're at it, what if Matthew Brady, Alexander Gardner, and Timothy O'Sullivan could have used modern cameras and film while they recorded the conflict? It was the time of the birth of photography, with its whatsit wagons and cumbersome equipment. Photographers didn't have the technology to capture moving images or even candid photographs. They needed exposures of many minutes, which explains why there are no photos of actual battles during the Civil War. But, through the spectacles created by reenacting, I have been able to do exactly that: capture the movement, excitement, and energy of a time past.

I consider myself extremely fortunate to have stumbled upon this form of performance art. That's what I think the reenactment of Civil War battles is—performance theater. When you walk into this world, you suspend disbelief. When I went to my first reenactment, in Spring Hill, Tennessee, back in 1995, I felt as if I had stepped back in time. I was so excited by the grandeur that I wasn't paying a lot of attention to my exposures, and I had shot half a roll before I discovered I was totally overexposed. Finally, I got myself together and got real lucky— I caught lightning in a fruit jar.

The reenactments represented in this photographic essay are not in chronological order. They are meant to be viewed as if they are of any battle, whether grand or small, a summation of the reenacting experience as seen through the eyes of a spectator. We start with the assemblage of troops as they marshal and get ready to do battle, from sitting around campfires to the continual drilling. The battles start and build to conclusions and it is back to marching and drilling and reflection on what has passed. And finally, the parades, and rejoicing and celebrations. The last image is of a memorial park, where heroes or cowards, great men or common, rest. They are all equal now.

# Introduction
## by Brian C. Pohanka

Forty years after the last shots were fired in America's bloodiest war, a retired lawyer named Frederick Lyman Hitchcock published a memoir recounting his Civil War service with the 132nd Pennsylvania Volunteers. A battle-scarred veteran of Antietam, Fredericksburg, and Chancellorsville, the horrific ordeal of those epic slaughters was indelibly seared upon his soul. He told of seeing a shell crush the body of a fellow officer "as though some giant had picked it up and furiously slammed it to the ground"—of a bullet splintering a comrade's arm "spattering my face with his warm blood"—of watching whole lines of charging troops "swept away as by a terrific whirlwind"—of "the horrible noise" of cannon fire and musketry, "the whizzing, singing, buzzing bullets" and powder smoke that "burned the coating of nose, throat and eyes almost like fire."

But for all the terrible drama of the battles he had passed through and so powerfully described, Frederick Hitchcock remembered the "chief event," the most "soul-stirring" experience of his wartime career, as President Lincoln's review of General Hooker's Army of the Potomac in the spring of 1863. The decades dropped away and the old veteran waxed euphoric as he recalled the awe-inspiring sight of thousands of soldiers, disciplined and proud, marching with "the poetry of rhythmic movement" like some vast, living thing.

"The quick, vigorous step, in rhythmical cadence to the music, the fife and drum, the massive swing, as though each man was actually a part of every other man; the glistening of bayonets like a long ribbon of polished steel, interspersed with the stirring effects of those historic flags, in countless numbers, made a picture beyond the power of description. A picture of the ages. How glad I am to have looked upon it. . . . I can still see that soul-thrilling column, that massive swing, those flaunting colors, that sheen of burnished steel! Majestic! Incomparable!! Glorious!!!"

"How can words describe the scene?" Hitchcock asked. "Look upon it; you shall never behold its like again."

And yet—as the remarkable images in this volume attest—135 years later it is in fact possible to behold soul-thrilling scenes of rhythmic ranks and burnished steel and flaunting banners that conjure up the pageantry of that wartime review. And, while thankfully lacking the horror, pain, and blood of war's brutal reality, we can still sniff the sulphurous musket smoke and hear the cannons roar as they did at Bull Run and Shiloh and Gettysburg. That we today can experience a tangible evocation of that vanished era is a consequence of the passionate affinity for past lives and events that inspires thousands of late-twentieth-century men, women, and children to don the garb of their nineteenth-century counterparts—and reenact the Civil War.

Even while the actual war between North and South still raged, commanders on occasion put their troops through simulated battles in which blank rounds were fired, and make-believe casualties littered the ground. More common were snowball fights of often epic proportions—entire brigades squaring off against their comrades in blue or gray with an enthusiasm that resulted in no small number of black eyes, broken teeth, and fractured bones. Perhaps the first true "Civil War reenactment" was held in August of 1878, when former Union General Judson Kilpatrick sponsored a mock battle between some 3,000 Union veterans—ironically cast as Confederates—and more than a thousand National Guard troops, who represented the Federal side. Nearly 40,000 spectators attended the event, which was staged on the fields of Kilpatrick's farm near Deckertown, New Jersey.

Over the years U.S. troops occasionally used Civil War battlefields as staging areas for war-game exercises, and portions of the Military Parks at Chickamauga and Gettysburg were commandeered as base camps for military instruction during the Spanish-American and First World Wars. But it was not until the advent of the Civil War Centennial in 1961 that the reenactment movement as we know it today took hold. That July 3,000 participants braved hundred-degree temperatures to reenact the first great clash between Yank and Reb at Bull Run, and similar commemorations on other battle anniversaries followed. These early reenactments left a great deal to be desired when it came to the accuracy of uniforms, weapons, accoutrements, and drill. But over time an interest in authenticity began to catch on—at first among a dedicated few who made an effort to study original clothing,

equipment, and tactical manuals—and a gradual but noticeable improvement could be observed in the quality as well as quantity of these re-created armies of the Union and Confederacy.

Far from proving a temporary fad, interest in Civil War reenacting continued unabated at the conclusion of the Centennial. Through the next three decades participation grew to proportions that few could have imagined in those early days of the hobby. During the 125th anniversary celebrations some 7,000 re-created the battle of Bull Run, and at Gettysburg in 1988 nearly 10,000 took part. Ten years later, the Antietam commemorations fielded 12,000 and Gettysburg in the neighborhood of 14,000 modern-day Union and Confederate soldiers. If one includes the many civilian participants, who assume the personas of farmers, nurses, refuges, and the like—not to mention the "sutlers" who craft and sell all manner of 1860s clothing and paraphernalia—1998's Gettysburg event featured something like 18,000 reenactors.

While a precise number is elusive, it has been estimated that today at least 30,000 people take part in Civil War reenactments on a regular basis—and some have placed the figure at nearly twice that number. Sizable cadres of American Civil War reenactors can be found in Britain, Germany, and Australia, and even the Ukraine—part of the former Soviet Union—hosts a small contingent. Reenactors come from all manner of backgrounds and professions. A given company might include lawyers, doctors, active duty or retired members of the military, students, policemen, construction workers—a literal cross-section of contemporary society.

What compels so many to assume the personas of those who passed through the fiery crucible of that "Tragic Era"? To spend thousands of dollars assembling their historical impression, and regularly travel hundreds of miles in order to spend a long weekend clad in the rough woolen garb of Yank and Reb—braving sweltering heat, or rain and mud or frost—sleeping on the ground in a canvas tent in some farmer's field? The reasons are as diverse as the individuals who participate in these huge re-creations.

Some reenactors have a direct ancestral connection to the Civil War and view their participation as a way of honoring their forebears' service in the cause of the Union or Confederacy. Some see their involvement as a healthy outdoor pastime that the whole family can participate in, a form of "theme camping," as it were. Many stress the educational aspects of their interest, both for themselves and the thousands of spectators who yearly witness their demonstrations. Very much in earnest, some eschew terms like "hobby" and "reenacting," preferring to call their activity "living history," and constantly striving to better the authenticity of their impression. Anyone who openly displays modern anachronisms in camp or otherwise fails to measure up, risks being scorned by the purists as a "farb"—a derisive appellation of obscure and debated origin, but a familiar term that dates to the earliest Centennial events.

Cutting across the various levels of background and knowledge and commitment is a heartfelt emotional bond with those who endured the tribulations of that war. It speaks of heritage and patriotism and idealism—and makes possible the suspension of disbelief that brings those long-dead people of the nineteenth century to life. As battlefields like Gettysburg and Chickamauga bear the likenesses of Civil War soldiers in granite and bronze, so modern-day Civil warriors can see themselves as "living monuments" to the men and women of that time.

My own involvement in Civil War living history began on an April morning in 1978 when I walked into the camp of the 5th New York Infantry as they prepared to take part in a reenactment of the battle of Sayler's Creek—one of the last engagements in Robert E. Lee's fateful march toward Appomattox Court House. I had assembled a passable Federal infantry uniform, was toting a Springfield rifled musket, and had the basic accoutrements to go with it. But I well remember how cold that night was, how flimsy my wool blanket seemed...and how many times I awoke shivering by the smoldering ashes of our campfire. I was eager but naive, and had a lot to learn; I was, in the parlance of the Civil War soldiers, a "fresh fish."

I've never regretted taking that step into the past. The friendships I've made, the lessons I've learned...and above all the insights I've gained have been of incalculable value to my understanding of, and empathy with the soldiers who waged that terrible war. When I read their letters, diaries or memoirs, or conduct research in libraries and archives in order to recount the history of their campaigns and battles—I can draw to some degree from my own experiences, and thereby relate to theirs.

Puffing my pipe and laughing with my pards by the crackling fireside; the flickering lights of hundreds of campfires on a chill autumn evening, fragments of music and song wafted on the breeze;

fog-shrouded hillsides in the half-light just before the dawn, with the pungent scent of wood smoke in the air; crawling out from a dog-tent's dubious shelter at the sound of reveille's jaunty fifes and drums, as bedraggled and sleepy-eyed soldiers fall in for their sergeant's roll call; the humble joy of that first tin cup of strong, hot coffee; stepping forward and ordering my company to "order arms, parade rest" during the solemn and inspirational ritual of dress-parade; pouring over *Hardee's* and *Casey's* tactical manuals in order to master the complex choreography of battalion drill, then seeing a regiment of six hundred men go through those very evolutions; taking pride in the company's performance of McClellan's intricate bayonet exercise; the smell of wet wool, the heft of the knapsack, the weight of musket or sword, even the sweat and dirt and grumbling—all of these things are honest, and real and true. I wonder how one can read about the Civil War, or write about the Civil War, and not want to experience these things?

Of course there are many things we can never experience, can never know, as they did. Above all, the blood and fear and ferocious carnage of those epic combats—whole ranks of men, marching elbow to elbow, geometric blocks of flesh and blood into the cauldron of battle, into the jaws of death. Most spectators attend these large events to see a "battle"; most reenactors travel to the events in order to participate in a "battle." And yet these "battles" are the least authentic thing we do, and by their very nature can lapse into theatricality, melodrama, and burlesque. It is hard to reconcile, and can be a troubling thought indeed for those of us who venerate and honor and love those bygone soldiers in blue and gray.

But as I looked through the striking photographs that appear in this book, I realized that even lacking the cruel reality inherent in war, mock battles do in fact convey a tangible and at times striking approximation of those combats in which horror and pageantry were inextricably, and to our modern view incomprehensibly, commingled. Even as the death toll mounted—ten, twenty, fifty thousand falling in a single engagement—the soldiers gazed upon such discipline and devotion with awe, and saw in it something that was glorious as well as terrible. Writing of the doomed Federal assault at Fredericksburg, Union officer Orlando Poe noted that "Men walked right up to their death as though it were to a feast." And watching as the Yankee columns reeled and crumpled but pressed on amid the deadly hail, Robert E. Lee is said to have remarked, "It is well war is so frightful, else we should grow too fond of it."

In his artful, atmospheric, and often inspirational images of Civil War reenactments, Kristoffersen has captured not only the humble moments of camp and field, but also the grandiose and panoramic scale of nineteenth-century warfare—something that the photographers of the Civil War era were themselves unable to accomplish. Talented as they were, Brady, Gardner, O'Sullivan, Gibson, Russell, and their fellow chroniclers were prevented—by the technical limitations and necessarily long exposure times of their bulky equipment—from recording movement. There are countless portraits of combatants, views of soldiers in camp, images of ravaged towns and scarred landscapes, and most shocking of all, the torn and bloated bodies of the fallen. But it was impossible for those mid-nineteenth-century photographers to document the marching columns, roiling smoke, and surging tides of fighting men in battle. Thanks to the fervent commitment of the reenactors, Kristoffersen has been able to capture at least an approximation of the terrible splendor of those battlefields—of serried ranks silhouetted against the vast, indifferent sky, advancing to death with an ardor born of belief.

Perhaps those of us for whom those four years of pain and glory hold such an abiding and compelling fascination can take solace in an oft-cited passage from the memoirs of Confederate veteran Berry Benson, a teenaged South Carolinian who passed through many a hard-fought engagement and lived to write eloquently of his wartime experiences.

"Who knows but again the old flags, ragged and torn, snapping in the wind, may face each other and flutter, pursuing and pursued, while the cries of victory fill a summer day? And after the battle, then the slain and wounded will arise, and all will meet together under the two flags, all sound and well, and there will be talking and laughter and cheers, and all will say: Did it not seem real? Was it not as in the old days?"

"It takes a raw recruit some time to learn that he is not to think or suggest, but obey . . . I acquired it at last, in humility and mud, but it was tough."

—*Pvt. Warren Lee Goss,* Massachusetts Volunteer

"However humble or unknown, they have renounced what are accounted pleasures and cheerfully undertaken all self-denials—privations, toils, dangers, sufferings, sicknesses, mutilations, life-long hurts and losses, death itself—for some great good, dimly seen but dearly held."

"The valley was filled with an impenetrable smoke like a dense fog and nothing for a little while could be seen but fire belching from the guns in various parts of the field. The noise was terrific, shaking the hills and reverberating through the valley, but loud above all was the exultant, fiendlike yell of the Confederate soldiers."

—*Sgt. Thomas Southwick*, 5th New York
at Gaines Mill, June 27, 1862

"The veil of smoke had slowly lifted and we could see the muzzles of the guns—their black and grim mouths pointed toward us. A horrid roar, then a shock that seemed to shake the very Earth. Then the dull thud of the balls as they tore their way through the bodies of the men—then the hiss of the grape—and the mingled screams of agony and rage. I looked around me. The ground was filled with the mangled dead and dying. . . ."

—*Pvt. Alexander Hunter*, 17th Virginia
at Second Manassas, August 30, 1862

"... it was a stand-up combat, dogged and unflinching, in a field almost bare.... the confronting lines looked into each other's faces at deadly range, less than one hundred yards apart, and they stood as immovable as the painted heroes in a battle-piece ... out in the sunlight, in the dying daylight, and under the stars they stood, and although they could not advance, they would not retire. There was some discipline in this, but there was much more of true valor."

—*Brigadier General William B. Taliaferro*, C.S.A.
on the battle of Brawner's Farm, August 28, 1862

"More than half a mile their front extends—more than a thousand yards the dull gray masses deploy, man touching man, rank pressing rank, and line supporting line. Their red flags wave; their horsemen gallop up and down; the arms of eighteen thousand men, barrel and bayonet, gleam in the sun, a sloping forest of flashing steel, through orchard, and meadow, and cornfield, magnificent, grim, irresistible. . ."

—*Capt. Frank A. Haskell,* Second Corps
on the Confederate assault, July 3, 1863, Gettysburg

And I saw askant the armies,
I saw as in noiseless dreams hundreds of battle-flags,
Borne through the smoke of the battles and pierc'd with
    missiles I saw them,
And carried hither and yon through the smoke, and torn
    and bloody,
And at last but a few shreds left on the staffs, (and all in
    silence,)
And the staffs all splinter'd and broken.

        —*Walt Whitman*
            "When Lilacs Last in the Door-Yard Bloom'd"
                      section 15

"Bands were playing, general and staff officers and gallant couriers were riding in front of and between the lines, 100 battle-flags were waving in the smoke of battle, and bursting shells were wreathing the air with great circles of smoke, while 20,000 brave men were marching in perfect order against the foe."

—*Colonel Ellison Capers*, 24th South Carolina
of the Confederate charge at Franklin, November 30, 1864

"I have seen soldiers die—I have been among them—may I say, *of them*—and I know it is not a fearful thing to fall on a field of glorious valor among the brave, though torn with the bolts of battle, and see the old flag go steadily on amidst the reeling lines. . . . Manhood asks no better death bed than that, nor is there any nearer Heaven."

—*General Joshua Lawrence Chamberlain*

"I think it is a noble and pious thing to do whatever we may by written word or moulded bronze and sculpted stone to keep our memories, our reverence and our love alive and to hand them on to new generations all too ready to forget."

—*Capt. Oliver Wendell Holmes,* 20th Massachusetts

Let us cross over the river and rest under the shade of the trees.

—*Stonewall Jackson*'s dying words
May 10, 1863

# Technical Data

These photographs were taken over a four-year period. Spring Hill, Tennessee, Shiloh, Tennessee, Antietam, Maryland, and Gettysburg, Pennsylvania, were the major reenactments covered, along with many other smaller battles I recorded from, Sacramento, Kentucky, to New York City, New York.

I have used a number of different cameras during the shooting of these images. My primary cameras have been Nikon N90s for the 35mm and Mamiya 7s for the medium format.

Various black-and-white films were used, with a special emphasis on Kodak and Konica infrared. Since I am making pictures of events long past I like the ethereal quality of these films. What my exposures and shutter speeds were, I can't tell you, because in the heat of battle, so to speak, I just go on instinct and experience.

All prints were printed on Ilford multigrade fiber–based paper, warm-toned.

# Acknowledgments

Being a freelance photographer is not the easiest job in the world. Many a time I have asked myself, what in the hell am I doing? Or why in the hell am I doing this? I hope these images will answer those questions.

Without the help and encouragement of friends and colleagues this book would not have been possible. Therefore a special thanks to Sven Larsen for his early contributions; thanks to Angie Sliger, Isgo Lepejian, Barrat Lepejian, and Jack Spencer for their help and their printing expertise. A very special thanks to Mac McGarvey for being my running buddy and pal; his enthusiasm and support were invaluable to me, especially on days when the humidity was close to a 100 percent. Last but not least, my mentor, agent, confidant, and friend, Michael Warlow, whose faith in me and my cameras has stood steadfast for as long as we have known each other.